Albrecht Dürer

Alix Wood

WINDMILL BOOKS
New York

Published in 2016 by **Windmill Books**, An Imprint of Rosen Publishing
29 East 21st Street, New York, NY 10010

Editor for Alix Wood Books: Eloise Macgregor
Designer: Alix Wood

Photo Credits: 4 © Prado Museum; 7 © The National Gallery; 9 bottom
© Metropolitan Museum of Art; 11 © nga/Horace Gallatin & Lessing
J. Rosenwald; 16 © nga/Rosenwald Collection; 23 © nga/David P. Tunick
& Elizabeth S. Tunick; 25 © nga/W.G. Russell Allen; 26-27 © nga/
Rosenwald Collection; 28, 29 © Shutterstock; all other images in the
public domain.

Cataloging-in-Publication Data
Wood, Alix.
Albrecht Dürer / by Alix Wood.
p. cm. — (Artists through the ages)
Includes index.
ISBN 978-1-4777-5595-2 (pbk.)
ISBN 978-1-4777-5594-5 (6 pack)
ISBN 978-1-4777-5448-1 (library binding)
1. Dürer, Albrecht, — 1471-1528 — Juvenile literature.
2. Painters — Germany — Biography — Juvenile literature.
I. Wood, Alix. II. Title.
ND588.D9 W66 2016
759.3'92—d23

Manufactured in the United States of America
CPSIA Compliance Information: Batch #W515PK:
For Further Information contact Windmill Books, New York, New York at 1-866-478-0556

Contents

Who Was Dürer?

Albrecht Dürer was born in 1471 in Nuremberg, Germany. He was one of eighteen children! His father was a **goldsmith**. His family moved to Germany from Hungary before he was born.

A **self-portrait**, age 22

Map of the World

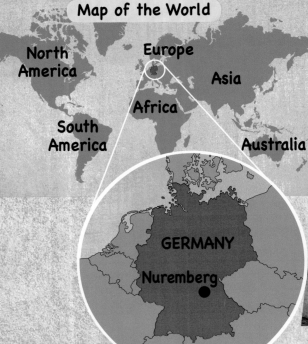

North America

Europe

Asia

Africa

South America

Australia

GERMANY

Nuremberg

Nuremberg, as it is today. Dürer lived in this square.

Dürer got his early education at a good school in St. Lorenz, Nuremburg. He also learned goldsmithing and drawing from his father. After a year, Dürer left the goldsmith shop and started his **apprenticeship** learning painting and **woodcut** design under Michael Wolgemut, a leading Nuremberg artist. He was an apprentice there for four years.

Young Dürer

Dürer did this self-portrait when he was just 13 years old. It was drawn using **silverpoint**, a technique that uses a thin rod of silver to make marks. Goldsmiths used silverpoint to draw their designs, so he probably learned this from his father. On it he wrote "This I have drawn from myself from the mirror, in the year 1484, when I was still a child."

A self-portrait, age 13

Travels Around Europe

After finishing his apprenticeship, Dürer spent some years traveling. He traveled through Germany, Switzerland, Austria, and back through France. He met other artists and saw many great paintings.

The Doors

When the Dürer family came from Hungary, the family name was Ajtos, which means "door" in Hungarian. Dürer's father chose the name Türer, as "tür" means door in German. The name changed to Dürer.

Dürer painted several **landscapes** and views while on his travels. This view is of a courtyard at Innsbruck castle, Austria.

The Painter's
Father, 1497

A Married Man

When Dürer was 23 years old he married Agnes Frey. She was the daughter of Hans Frey, a friend of his parents. Frey was a reasonably wealthy man who made jewelry and musical instruments and it was thought the two would be a good match.

The marriage helped raise Dürer's **status** and gave him enough money to help set up his own workshop. Dürer sketched his future bride Agnes, right, who was just a teenager. He captures her with just a few strokes of the pen.

Dürer wrote "My Agnes" under his sketch, 1494

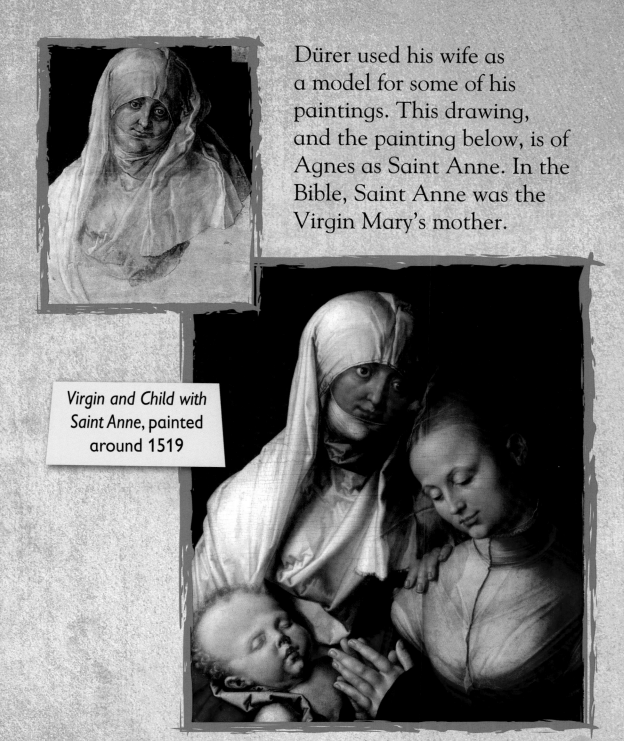

Dürer used his wife as a model for some of his paintings. This drawing, and the painting below, is of Agnes as Saint Anne. In the Bible, Saint Anne was the Virgin Mary's mother.

Virgin and Child with Saint Anne, painted around 1519

Woodcuts and Prints

Dürer worked hard in his new workshop. He set up his own printing press and produced his own illustrated books from the Bible, using prints made from woodcuts. Dürer was the best woodcut artist in Europe at the time.

A woodcut print is made by drawing on a wood block, and then cutting around the design so that the drawing is left sticking up out of the wood. If you roll ink onto the block and press it down on paper, you get a printed copy. To get the printed image to appear the right way, the artist must do the drawing backwards!

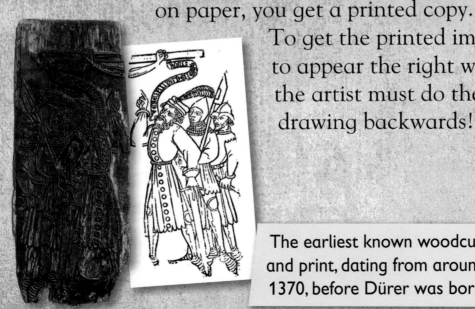

The earliest known woodcut and print, dating from around 1370, before Dürer was born

Dürer's *The Four Horsemen of the Apocalypse*, 1498, is considered one of the best woodcuts ever made.

Painting Nature

Dürer's father died in 1502 and he had to care for his ill mother. Dürer and his wife would sell prints of his work at local fairs. All the work he had put into his woodcuts in the years before meant his prints could provide him with a small income now. It was a difficult time and Dürer's own health suffered. To entertain himself he painted some beautiful watercolors of nature.

Signed

In Dürer's time, animals were not subjects for serious art. The fact that Dürer signed this watercolor *Young Hare* shows that he valued it as an artwork and not just a **sketch.**

Dürer created this detailed watercolor of a clump
of grass and weeds! He once said "beauty lies even
in humble, perhaps ugly things." This work is the
earliest ever realistic painting of plant life.

Altarpieces

Dürer visited Italy in 1505. He was asked to paint an altarpiece for the Church of San Bartolomeo, Venice, by some German merchants there. The finished painting *The Feast of the Rosary* includes the Pope kneeling on the left, and the German emperor Maximillian I kneeling on the right.

Dürer liked to paint himself into his paintings. Look at the man standing by the tree on the right looking out of the painting at the viewer. Dürer used his self-portrait to "sign" the painting. His scroll says: "Albrecht Dürer, a German, produced it within the span of five months. 1506." Many artists put themselves in their work after Dürer.

An Art Jigsaw Puzzle

Dürer's 1504 *Jabach Altarpiece* once had three panels which became separated. Despite now being different shapes, these two panels are part of the jigsaw. See how the dress runs across both pictures. The other panel is still missing. Can you spot Dürer?

Copper Engravings

Dürer perfected the art of copper engraving. A sheet of copper is covered in a thin layer of wax and then drawn on with a needle. The plate is then dipped in acid, which eats away the copper the wax was removed from. The rest of the wax is then removed and the plate can be used for printing.

Dürer created some of the world's best engravings. Look closely at the date on this engraving. Dürer corrected it from 1505 to 1508. He must have started it before he went to Italy and finished it on his return.

Saint George on Horseback, 1508

Saint Jerome in his Study, 1514

Using Blue Paper

When Dürer was in Italy, he tried the local blue Venetian paper to create some of his drawings and sketches. The effects the paper gave were beautiful. Dürer drew the highlights in white paint and the shadows in black ink, and the blue of the paper created the rest of the image. The drawings look almost as if the image is coming out of the paper!

Making Do

When Dürer returned to Nuremberg he couldn't find any of the blue paper. Dürer created his own blue tones by painting his paper first instead. One of his most famous works, *Praying Hands*, right, was created in this way.

Dürer used the blue paper to create sketches for his paintings. The sketch *Head of the Twelve Year Old Christ*, right, was used to create the young Jesus figure he painted in the work below.

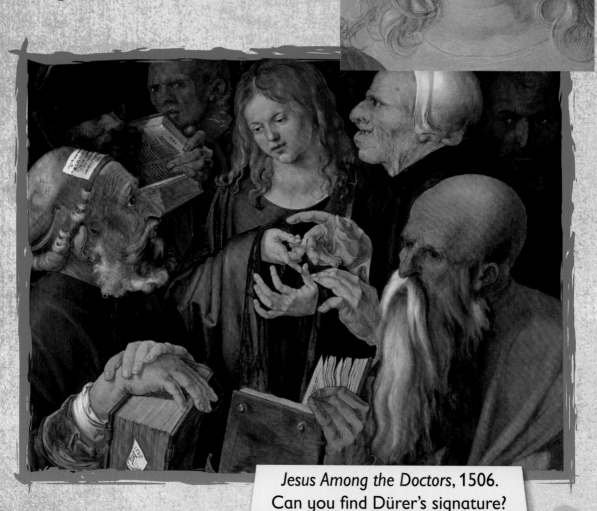

Jesus Among the Doctors, 1506. Can you find Dürer's signature?

Dürer and Math

During Dürer's visits to Italy he met Luca Pacioli, a mathematician who had written about how shapes such as the human form could be divided up mathematically. He also met artist Jacopo de Barbari who was interested in how math could be used in art.

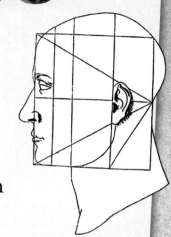

Dürer went on to write math books on shapes and **proportions**. One of his famous engravings, *Melancholia*, right, has an interesting shaped stone on the left that has puzzled mathematicians for years! It looks like it should mean something, but no one is quite sure what!

Magic Square

In the top right corner of *Melancholia* is a magic square. Each row, column, and quarter add up to 34. The square also cleverly includes the date of the painting, 1514.

Melancholia, 1514

Painting for the Emperor

In 1512, emperor Maximillian I visited Nuremberg. He met Dürer and asked him to create the woodcut on page 23. Pleased with the result, Maximillian gave Dürer a yearly pension and asked him to paint his portrait.

Dürer met the emperor and did a pencil sketch which he turned into this painting. Dürer worked for Maximillian I until the emperor died in 1519, producing drawings, woodcuts, and etchings.

Portrait of Maximillian I, 1519

The Triumphal Arch is one of the largest prints ever produced, at over 11.5 feet (3.5 m) tall! It is made up of 195 separate woodblocks. The detailed drawing is full of references to the life of Maximillian I.

a close-up of a colored print

The Master Prints

The engraving on the right, *Knight, Death, and the Devil* is believed to **symbolize** faithfulness. The knight and his faithful dog are riding a steady route past death (holding the **hourglass**) and the horned devil (right).

Knight, Death, and the Devil is thought to be one of a series of three engravings known as *The Master Prints*. The other two are *Saint Jerome in his Study* on page 17 and *Melancholia* on page 21. The three prints are thought to represent being active, thoughtful, and sad. Which do you think is which? However, there is no real evidence that they were ever treated or sold together as a set.

A Set?

The three master prints are almost identical in size, and each features a skull, a dog, and an hourglass. Can you find them? *Melancholia* is tricky. The skull shape is drawn on the stone.

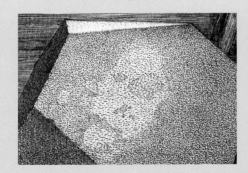

The Rhinoceros

In 1515, no one in Europe had seen a rhinoceros. One animal was sent by ship as a gift from the ruler of Gujarat, India, to the king of Portugal. When news of this incredible creature reached Germany, Dürer wanted to draw it. He had very little information about what it looked like. He was told it was the color of a speckled turtle and was covered with thick scales.

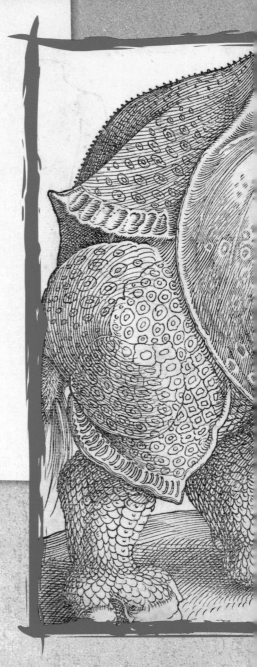

Dürer did not get his rhinoceros drawing quite right. It doesn't really have scaly legs or armor plates! Even so, for the next 300 years Dürer's picture was printed in books to show what a rhinoceros looked like!

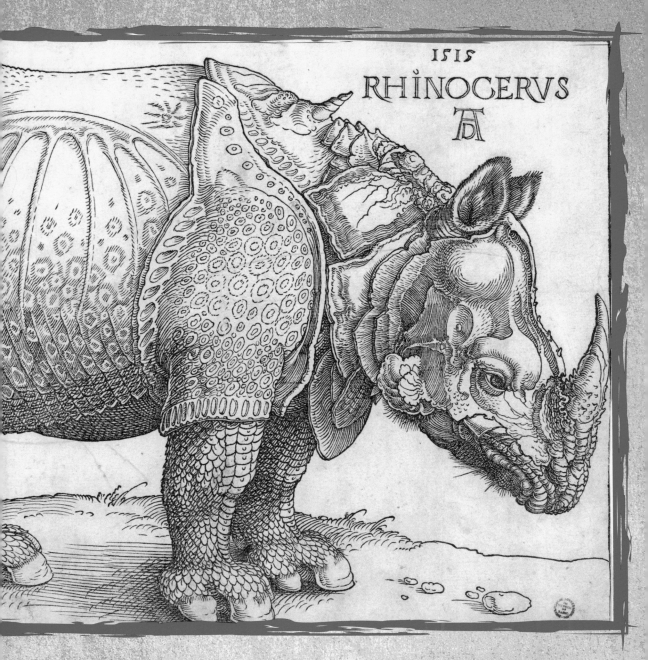

1515
RHINOCERVS

Sadly, Dürer's love of animals led to him catching malaria when walking in a swamp looking for a stranded whale. He died of the disease years later.

Dürer's Legacy

Dürer died in 1528 at age 56. He is remembered as a talented painter, printmaker, and author of several books on the **theory** of art. He was unusual among artists as he was famous during his lifetime, as well as after his death.

As well as being an outstanding artist, Dürer brought several new subjects to the world of art. He introduced the idea of the self-portrait, and painted the earliest pure landscapes to have survived in the history of western art. He painted unusual subjects such as the wing (opposite), which no one would have thought was a suitable subject before.

A statue of Dürer in Nuremberg

ALBRECHT DÜRER

The Wing of
a Blue Roller,
1512

Dürer's House

Dürer's house in Nuremberg has been turned into a museum of his life and work.

Glossary

apprenticeship
(uh-PREN-tis-ship)
A period in which a young person works with another person to learn a skill or trade.

goldsmith
(GOHLD-smith)
A person who makes or sells articles of gold.

hourglass (OW-er-glas)
A timekeeper that has two parts connected by a narrow neck, in which sand takes one hour to fall from the upper part to the lower part.

landscapes
(LAND-skaypz)
Pictures of the natural scenery.

proportions
(pruh-POR-shunz)
Measurements of one part compared to another.

self-portrait
(self–POR-tret)
A picture done by the artist of himself or herself.

silverpoint (SIL-ver-POYNT)
Drawing with a silver-pointed instrument on paper prepared with a coating of powdered bone or zinc whites.

sketch (SKECH)
A quick drawing.

status (STAA-tuss)
Position or rank in relation to others.

symbolize (SIM-buh-lyz)
To stand for something else.

theory (THEER-ee)
An idea or group of ideas that tries to explain something.

woodcut (WUHD-kut)
A wood carving that can create a picture by rubbing charcoal or other art materials against it and pressing it to paper.

Websites

For web resources related to the subject of this book, go to: **www.windmillbooks.com/weblinks** and select this book's title.

Read More

Civardi, Anne. *Action! Movement in Art*. London: Wayland, 2005.

Kramer, Ann. *Artists*. London: Franklin Watts, 2007.

Thomson, Leo. *Place and Space: Landscapes in Art*. London: Wayland, 2005.

Index